ROYAL CASTLE

The Inside Story of Windsor

John Farndon

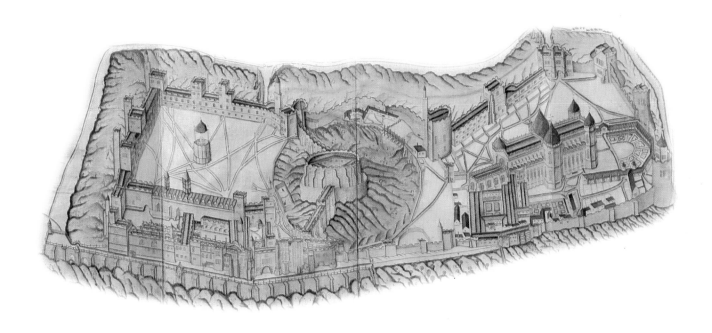

 A Royal Collection Book

VIKING
Published by the Penguin Group
Penguin Books Ltd, 27 Wrights Lane, London W8 5TZ, England
Penguin Books USA Inc., 375 Hudson Street, New York, New York 10014, USA
Penguin Books Australia Ltd, Ringwood, Victoria, Australia
Penguin Books Canada Ltd, 10 Alcorn Avenue, Toronto, Ontario, Canada M4V 3B2
Penguin Books (NZ) Ltd, 182–190 Wairau Road, Auckland 10, New Zealand

Penguin Books Ltd, Registered Offices: Harmondsworth, Middlesex, England

First published 1997
1 3 5 7 9 10 8 6 4 2

Acknowledgements

We are indebted to a large number of people who have given us their knowledge and time to help create this book.

We would like to give especial thanks to Royal Collection Enterprises and all the many individuals from the Royal Collection who have helped us.

The following have also given invaluable help and advice:
Steven Brindle, Inspector of Ancient Monuments and Historic Buildings, English Heritage; the Dean and Canons of Windsor; Donald W. Insall and Associates, Chartered Architects; Dan Newman; Dr Geoffrey Parnell, Keeper of Tower History, Royal Armouries.

The publisher would like to thank the following for their kind permission to reproduce illustrations:
Ancient Art and Architecture Collection (Ronald Sheridan's Photo-Library): 7 top c/top r.
With special authorization of the City of Bayeux, Musée de la Tapisserie, Bayeux/Giraudon/Bridgeman Art Library, London: 4 top l/centre/below l,
5 top l/top r/below.
Bibliothèque de L'Arsenal, Paris/Bridgeman Art Library, London: 20 below (The marriage of Renaud of Montauban and Clarisse/*Liedet*,Loyset)
Bibliothèque Nationale, Paris/Bridgeman Art Library: 21 top r ('De Claris Mulieribus' Works of Giovanni Boccaccio).
British Library, London/Bridgeman Art Library: Luttrell Psalter 6(Add 42130 f.54), 10(Add 42130 f.147v), 14 centre/bottom(Add 42130 f.207v),
22 top(Add 42130 f.163v); 19 top l Geoffrey Chaucer (Add 5141 f 1); 20 top l Christine de Pisan writing at her desk (Harl 4431 f.4); 21 below (April, Book of Hours c.
1520 - Add 24098 f.21v); 27 top r (G11631.BL Title page of Shakespeare's Comedies, Histories and Tragedies).
British Museum, London: 24 below (Marcus Gheeraerts The Elder, 1576 etching)/E.T. Archive, 37 top l (Le Mort).
The Dean and Canons of Windsor: 6 top c, 19 centre r, 24 top l, 25.
E.T. Archive: 18 centre.
Ecole des Beaux-Arts, Paris/Bridgeman Art Library, London: 21 centre (Industry/*Bourdichon*, Jean).
Mary Evans Picture Library: 4 top c, 26 top l, 27 centre r.
Museum of London: 15 top r/centre r/bottom r.
Osterreichische Nationalbibliothek, Vienna/Bridgeman Art Library: 18/19 centre.
Private Collection/Bridgeman Art Library: 18 top l/r, 19 top centre Ellesmere Manuscript (Facsimile Edition 1911) Canterbury Tales,
32 below l (Oliver Cromwell by *Cooper*, Samuel)
Copyright © 1997 The Royal Collection, Her Majesty Queen Elizabeth II: 12, 13, 19 top r (Henry VIII Gateway, *Sandby*), 24 (Survey of Honour of Windsor/*Norden*, J.,
St George's Chapel/*Wild*, Charles), 26 below (Queen Elizabeth I/*Hilliard*, Nicholas), 27 below, 28, 29, 30 top/below, 31(King Charles I's Shakespeare, King Charles I
testimonial for Sir Thomas Herbert), 32 top (Hugh May/*Cooper*, Samuel), 34, 35, 36, 37 top r/below, 38, 39, 44, 45, 46, 47 (centre photo Donald W. Insall and
Associates).The Royal Archives © 1997 Her Majesty Queen Elizabeth II: 42 top l.

Illustrator Credits
Gino D'Achille – Artist Partners: 6/7, 14/15, 26/27, 28/29, 30/31.
Bill Gregory – Artist Partners: 4/5 Map.
Chris West – Black Hat Ltd: 4 (Soldiers fighting), 19 (Man in stocks), 22/23, 42/43.
Robert Calow – Eikon: 10/11, 20/21.
Mike Foster and Carl Venton – Maltings Partnership: 8/9, 16/17, 32/33, 40/41.

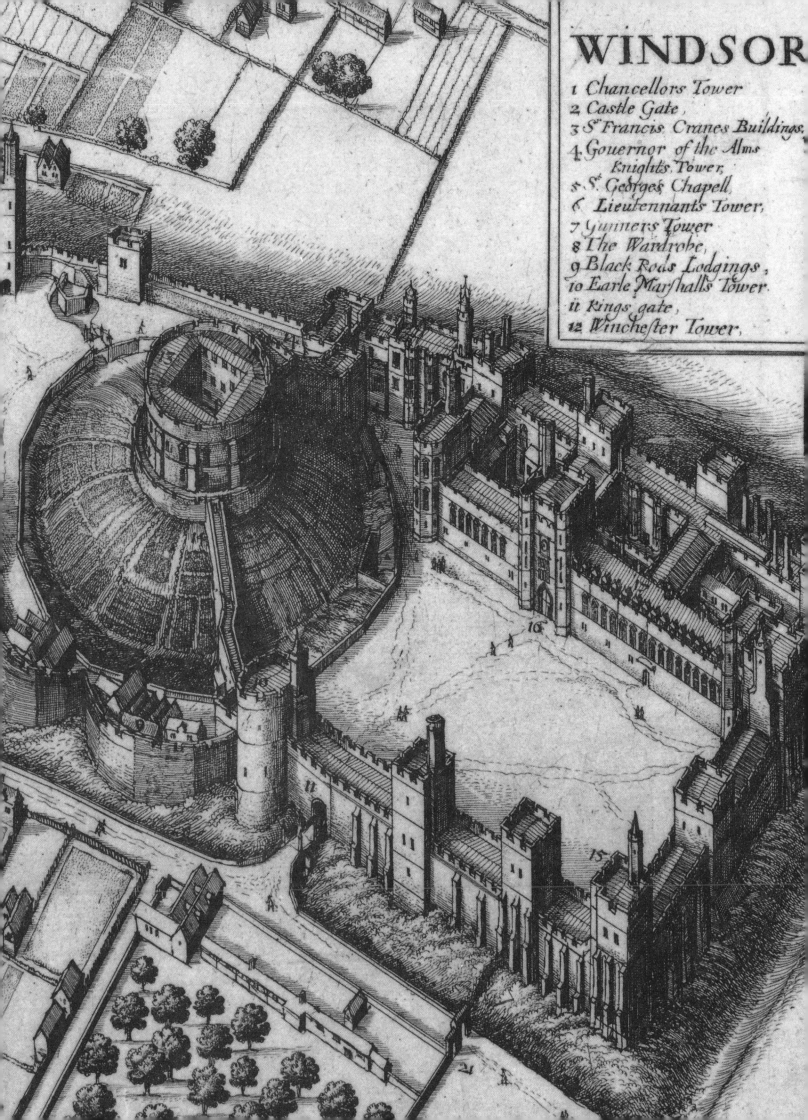

WINDSOR

1 Chancellors Tower
2 Castle Gate.
3 S.t Francis. Cranes Buildings.
4 Gouernor of the Alms
   Knights. Tower.
5 S.t Georges Chapell.
6 Lieutennants Tower.
7 Gunners Tower.
8 The Wardrobe.
9 Black Rods Lodgings.
10 Earle Marshalls Tower.
11 Kings gate.
12 Winchester Tower.

Contents

Fortifying Britain

On Christmas Day 1066, a sullen crowd gathered outside the great new Abbey of Westminster. On the Abbey steps, guards eyed them warily, swords drawn. Inside, a new king was being crowned. But this new king was not the son of the dead king, Harold. He was not even English. He was William the Conqueror, leader of the Norman invaders who had swept over from France in the autumn, crushing Harold's army at Hastings and capturing London. The Normans' grip on power, though, was still weak and the guards on the Abbey steps were nervous.

Suddenly, a shout in English went up inside, hailing the new king. The guards, who spoke only French, were sure things had gone wrong. They hurled themselves on the crowd and set fire to nearby houses. In the chaos, only a few people were left to witness the coronation. But from that moment William became King William I, and he soon set about building mighty castles all over England to strengthen his hold over his new kingdom. The invading army moved through England throwing up wooden castles as they went.

William the Conqueror
William was a ruthless soldier who ruled England for twenty years after conquering it. When he died in 1087, his son, also called William, became king.

Harold at Court
In the days before the Norman invasion, the English king, Harold Godwin, held court at Winchester in the kingdom of Wessex.

Axe v sword
In battle, knights wore protective coats of chain mail (linked iron rings) called hauberks and had wooden shields. But while the Norman knights fought with swords, the English knights (or housecarls) preferred battleaxes.

In Wales, the Normans made only piecemeal conquests, and built castles along the border.

Exeter

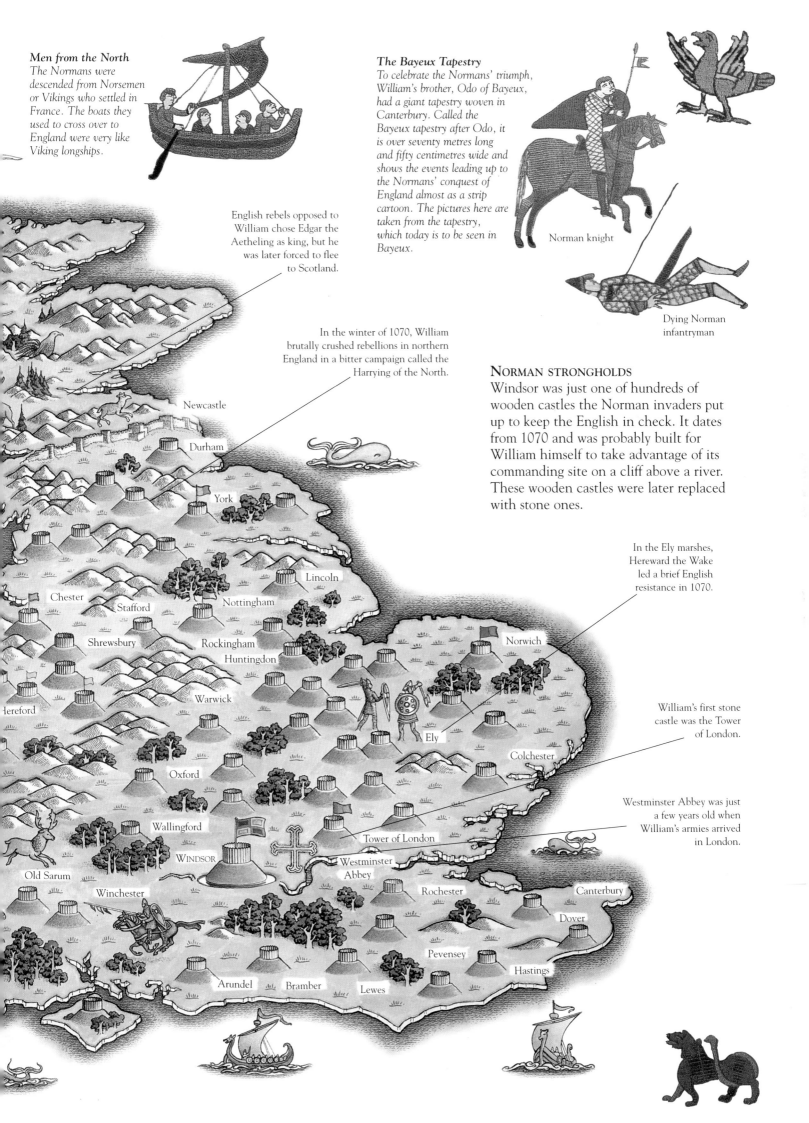

Men from the North
The Normans were descended from Norsemen or Vikings who settled in France. The boats they used to cross over to England were very like Viking longships.

The Bayeux Tapestry
To celebrate the Normans' triumph, William's brother, Odo of Bayeux, had a giant tapestry woven in Canterbury. Called the Bayeux tapestry after Odo, it is over seventy metres long and fifty centimetres wide and shows the events leading up to the Normans' conquest of England almost as a strip cartoon. The pictures here are taken from the tapestry, which today is to be seen in Bayeux.

Norman knight

Dying Norman infantryman

English rebels opposed to William chose Edgar the Aetheling as king, but he was later forced to flee to Scotland.

In the winter of 1070, William brutally crushed rebellions in northern England in a bitter campaign called the Harrying of the North.

NORMAN STRONGHOLDS
Windsor was just one of hundreds of wooden castles the Norman invaders put up to keep the English in check. It dates from 1070 and was probably built for William himself to take advantage of its commanding site on a cliff above a river. These wooden castles were later replaced with stone ones.

In the Ely marshes, Hereward the Wake led a brief English resistance in 1070.

William's first stone castle was the Tower of London.

Westminster Abbey was just a few years old when William's armies arrived in London.

Newcastle

Durham

York

Lincoln

Chester

Stafford

Nottingham

Shrewsbury

Rockingham

Huntingdon

Hereford

Warwick

Norwich

Ely

Colchester

Oxford

Wallingford

WINDSOR

Tower of London

Westminster Abbey

Old Sarum

Winchester

Rochester

Canterbury

Dover

Pevensey

Hastings

Arundel

Bramber

Lewes

Wooden Walls

THERE WERE JUST a handful of castles in England before the Normans came. The Normans realized that castles were an effective way of establishing their control. As they were in a hostile land and in a hurry, they had no time to stop and build in stone. Instead, they worked with earth and wood. To start with, they protected their troop camps with ditches and fences of wooden stakes. As they fanned out across the country, they began to choose strategic and easy-to-defend sites. They would dig a ditch and pile up a high mound of earth inside it called a motte, which could be defended by just a handful of men. Around the motte they would create a large flat area called a bailey, surrounded by a fence of wooden stakes and another ditch. The motte-and-baileys were the first real castles. William built one at Windsor, where a chalk cliff gave a commanding view of the approach to London from the west. It was also a good base for hunting in the nearby forests. It became one of a ring of fortresses the Normans built around London, each thirty kilometres – a day's march – from the capital.

Ship in stone
Among the earliest stone buildings at Windsor was the chapel and its vestry (now called the Dean's Chapel). Carved in the stone passageway between the chapel and the vestry is this remarkable piece of medieval graffito, showing a ship called a balinger.

BUILDING A MOTTE-AND-BAILEY
Digging out the ditch and piling up the mound required a huge amount of labour. But the Normans were few, so they must have forced local men to help them. Windsor is one of the biggest Norman fortresses and it was probably laid out by William FitzOsbern, ruler of the Isle of Wight, the great military engineer who also created the castles of Arundel, Carisbrooke and Rockingham.

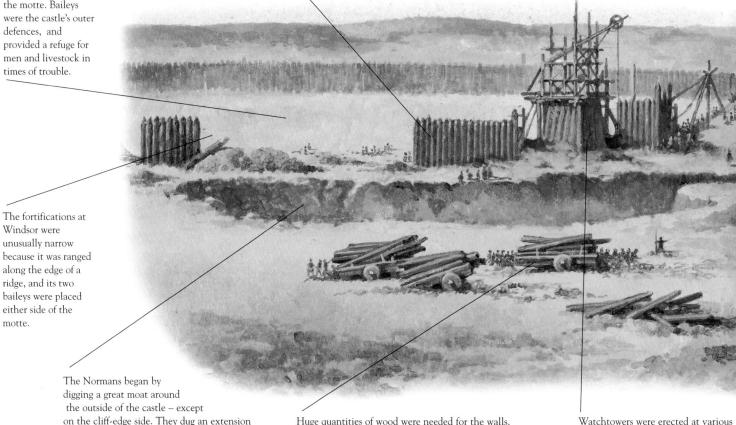

Norman castles had anything from one to six baileys – wide level areas of the fort below the motte. Baileys were the castle's outer defences, and provided a refuge for men and livestock in times of trouble.

All the defensive walls were wooden stockades – except for the vulnerable main gate, which may have been built in stone.

The fortifications at Windsor were unusually narrow because it was ranged along the edge of a ridge, and its two baileys were placed either side of the motte.

The Normans began by digging a great moat around the outside of the castle – except on the cliff-edge side. They dug an extension loop to this moat around the castle mound.

Huge quantities of wood were needed for the walls. It was probably brought by cart from the local forests.

Watchtowers were erected at various points around the perimeter fence.

Ball and chain mace, 1300s
In the Middle Ages, vicious maces like these, adapted from grain-threshing tools, were used to batter armour.

Anglo-Saxon sword
Among the conquered Anglo-Saxons, only chieftains had swords. They were used for slashing rather than thrusting.

The watchtower was put up with the aid of scaffolding and winches.

The motte was crowned with a wooden tower. This was raised on stilts and acted both as a lookout tower and a last refuge or keep.

The top of the mound was surrounded by a stockade of logs, firmly fixed together.

The only way into the motte was across a sloping bridge, perched on high pillars.

The slope of the mound may have been covered in slippery clay to make it hard for enemies to climb.

The mound was gradually built up in layers, each topped by interlinked stones and beaten earth.

The castle mound or motte was slowly built up with all the chalk dug out from the moats.

Labourers wound their way up the mound carrying baskets of chalk soil.

7

Under Siege

THROUGHOUT the summer of 1216, Windsor proved its strength as a castle. For three long months just sixty knights loyal to King John held the castle against a ferocious assault by a great army of rebel barons and their French allies. The barons were rebelling against King John because the previous summer at nearby Runnymede John had agreed to their demands in a charter called the Magna Carta – but then sent the Pope such a misleading story about the charter that the Pope cancelled it. The angry barons rose in rebellion and within a few weeks had captured nearly all John's castles in southern England. Only Dover and Windsor stood firm.

Besides building massive stone walls, Henry II built a great stone tower on top of the castle mound which was now firm enough to support the weight. This tower, called the Great Tower, was rebuilt and heightened in the nineteenth century to make the much taller Round Tower.

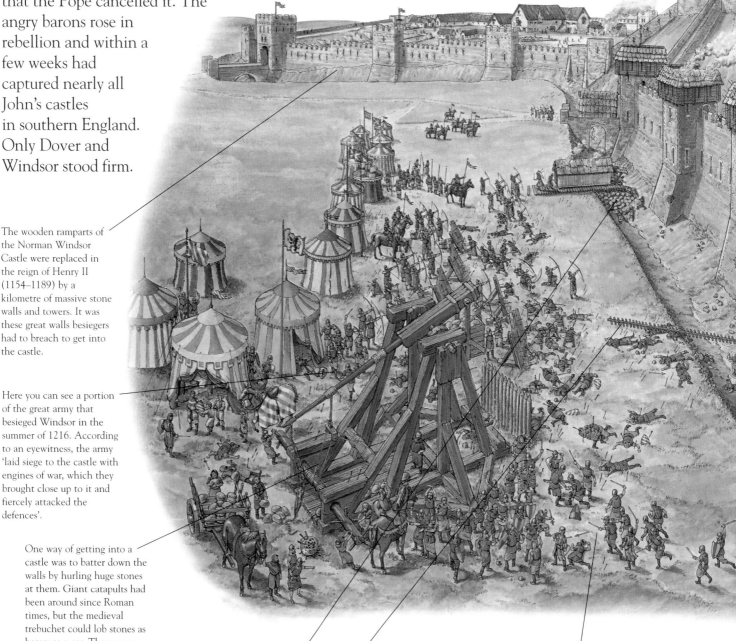

The wooden ramparts of the Norman Windsor Castle were replaced in the reign of Henry II (1154–1189) by a kilometre of massive stone walls and towers. It was these great walls besiegers had to breach to get into the castle.

Here you can see a portion of the great army that besieged Windsor in the summer of 1216. According to an eyewitness, the army 'laid siege to the castle with engines of war, which they brought close up to it and fiercely attacked the defences'.

One way of getting into a castle was to batter down the walls by hurling huge stones at them. Giant catapults had been around since Roman times, but the medieval trebuchet could lob stones as heavy as a car. There were probably four of these great catapults at the siege of Windsor.

The ditch around the castle was a vital part of its defences. Its steep sides and muddy bottom made it very difficult for attackers trying to get scaling ladders up. To get siege towers and battering rams up against the walls, besiegers first had to fill in the ditch.

Another way of getting into the castle was to scale the walls – but attackers on ladders faced a constant barrage of stones, hot water and arrows from the defenders on the walls above. The besiegers may have built a belfry – this was a giant tower on wheels that could be rolled up against the walls. It was hung with wet skins to protect it from flaming arrows and had a drawbridge at the top from which men could leap on to the castle walls.

Twice, the ropes of the besieging army's great catapults were cut by daring raids led by Engelard de Cygony. Engelard crept out under cover of darkness through secret passages called sally ports, which emerged beyond the castle ditch. One of these sally ports was rediscovered earlier this century.

WINDSOR BESIEGED

Windsor withstood all the rebel barons' efforts to take it. After three months, they simply gave up and went off in pursuit of King John. The rebellion ended when John died in October, from, it is said, eating too many peaches and drinking too much cider.

Defending the castle against the rebel barons was a garrison of sixty knights under the command of the Constable, Engelard de Cygony. Engelard was said to be 'very skilful in the art of war', and the barons feared him so much that they had insisted on a clause in the Magna Carta banishing him from the realm. He certainly proved his courage in the siege, twice leading his men in daring raids on the attackers, and holding the castle against tremendous odds.

In 1216, the royal apartments were in a two-storey stone block up against the north wall of the castle. Here, along with the King's Hall, were the pantry and buttery, the King's Chamber, the wardrobe and a chapel around a cloistered herb garden. The great kitchen was in much the same place as it is today.

Windsor had square towers like most other castles of the time. But while Windsor was under siege from King John's enemies, John launched a successful attack on Rochester Castle by undermining the corners of the towers. This showed how vulnerable the corners of square towers could be. When the western defences were completed by John's son, Henry III, the new towers were D-shaped.

To drive defending bowmen from the walls, attacking bowmen needed to get in close. So a group of them would move in behind a wooden shield on wheels called a mantlet. Sometimes, bowmen had individual shields called pavises.

Direct assaults on well-defended castles rarely worked. Even hundreds of metres away from the castle, attackers were in danger from arrows and crossbow bolts. Closer in, flaming torches of pitch-soaked rope, boiling water and stones would be dropped from the battlements. The defenders had their own catapults too, and hurled boulders.

Hand-to-hand fighting only took place when raiding parties emerged from the castle to try to disrupt the long, slow siege process.

In time of war, the castle walls were topped with wooden hoardings which jutted out on beams from the wall. Holes between the beams allowed defenders to hurl things down on attackers at the foot of the castle wall, where they were out of reach of arrows. Although the wooden roof protected the defenders in the hoardings, it was highly vulnerable to catapults and flaming arrows.

Mighty Defences

ROYAL CASTLES had a special role in the medieval world. A baron's private castle might be just a fortified home, but the king used his castles to enforce his power across the land. To discourage rebellion, royal castles were garrisoned by soldiers at all times; private castles were often left in the hands of just a few domestics. Windsor was one of sixty royal castles in England garrisoned throughout the reign of Edward II (1307–1327). Castles were costly to build, but a good stone castle could be defended by a handful of knights and men-at-arms. The key to its defences were high towers that gave the defenders a clear view over the surrounding land and stone walls up to seven metres thick. Both walls and towers were topped by battlements – low walls with gaps for defenders to rain missiles down on the enemy. But castle design was always changing. As besiegers invented ever more ingenious ways of attacking, so castles evolved from a simple square tower to elaborate rings of fortifications, and the gatehouse became equipped with all kinds of fiendish traps for the intruder.

THE GATEHOUSE
The entrance was the castle's weakest point, so it had to be equipped with all kinds of devices for keeping the enemy out. Gatehouse designs varied considerably, but Windsor probably had a single tower gatehouse like the one shown here. Others had twin towers, one on either side of the gate arch.

Tortoise
To batter down the castle gate or start mining operations, soldiers attacking a castle had to get to the walls under a hail of defenders' arrows. To protect themselves, they advanced under a roof of skins and wood called a tortoise – or sometimes a cat, because when mounted on wheels it crept forward very slowly.

Big sling
Of all the siege engines at the besiegers' disposal, few were more deadly than the sling called the trebuchet. Brought to England by the French in 1217, trebuchets were remarkably powerful and accurate. The biggest trebuchets could hurl boulders the weight of a car hundreds of metres with devastating accuracy. Their counter-weighting system was so refined that they could hit the same spot again and again. At the siege of Montsegur in France in 1244, one hurled forty-kilogram missiles at the same point in the wall day and night every twenty minutes until it crumbled.

Here the castle ditch is spanned by a stone bridge, but some castles had a drawbridge or turning bridge. This was a wooden bridge that pivoted like a huge see-saw and could be swung up into the castle to stop the enemy getting in.

Little sling
Probably dating back to Roman times, mangons and mangonels were used by the Normans throughout the eleventh and twelfth centuries. They were smaller than trebuchets, but could still hurl 20-kilogram boulders over 200 metres.

Battering ram
One way through the gate was to batter it down. Rams were brought up against the gate by soldiers under a protective roof like a tortoise. The ram was a long wooden beam with an iron head suspended by chains.

The portcullis or drop-gate was a heavy oak gate with iron spikes on the bottom which dropped vertically through slots.

The portcullis was wound up slowly on ropes and pulleys. But it could be dropped shut instantly by knocking a wedge away – crushing anyone underneath with its massive weight or impaling them on its iron spikes.

The portcullis opened on to a narrow tunnel. Attackers getting through would be bombarded by stones, quick-lime and boiling water rained down on them through holes called murder holes.

Belfry

Belfrys were tall wooden towers on wheels. Sometimes they were rolled up against the castle walls so that attackers could jump on to the battlements. More often, they were used as a platform for archers and catapults to shoot down on to the castle walls. They were sometimes big enough for 200 archers and a dozen catapults.

On top of the castle wall was a parapet protected by battlements. Battlements were walls about a metre high with gaps called crenels for archers to fire through. In between each crenel was a higher section of wall called a merlon, where the archer could hide to reload.

Archers stood behind an opening in the wall called an embrasure, which tapered to a narrow slit or loop. The archer could aim and fire through this slit without exposing himself to enemy arrows. Longbowmen had tall narrow loops; crossbowmen had broader shorter loops. Not all loops were for bowmen: some were just windows for light and air.

Sapping the castle's strength

One feared method of attack was the mine or sap. Sappers dug a tunnel under the castle. The tunnel roof was supported by timber props, but once they had made a big hole beneath a tower, they would set the props on fire, the hole would collapse and the tower would come crashing down.

Most castles were surrounded by a ditch, but in the thirteenth century these were dug deeper and filled with water. This moat was the only sure defence against sapping.

11

Knights in Armour

THE LYNCHPINS in the defence of a castle like Windsor were knights. Knights were the elite fighting men, highly trained in combat both on horseback and on foot. They always wore armour and generally rode into battle on horseback. They also had a strict code of honour, called chivalry, from *chevalier*, the French word for horseman.

Becoming a knight was a long and expensive process, so most knights were rich noblemen. A young boy who was to become a knight was generally sent off at the age of seven as a page to an uncle or great lord who would teach him how to behave and how to ride. At fourteen, he became the knight's squire (apprentice), learning both how to handle weapons and also how to look after his master's armour, dress him for battle and serve his food. If he passed all the tests, a squire was finally made a knight at the age of twenty-one or so, in a ceremony called dubbing.

A KNIGHT'S ARMOUR

The first suits of armour were simply shirts of mail, made from hundreds of tiny linked rings of iron. Gradually, steel plates were added to protect limbs and shoulders. By the 1400s, most knights wore full suits of plate armour. Suits like these were hot, weighing twenty to twenty-five kilograms, and knights had to be fit to run and fight in them.

Vamplate
By the late sixteenth century, full armour was used only for show and for tilting. Armour for the tilt was different in a number of ways to battle armour. This is the vamplate from Prince Henry's suit of armour of 1610. It protects the hand which holds the lance. The lance goes through the hole in the middle.

The upper body was protected by the cuirass, consisting of a breastplate and a backplate held together by leather straps.

Knights' horses often had elaborate coats and decoration. This medieval-style decoration, though, is entirely modern.

The thistle, Tudor rose and fleur-de-lis decorations, seen on this armour, are all emblems of the royal household.

Jousts involved knights charging each other with lances across a barrier known as a tilt. When tilting, knights often wore an extra piece of armour on the target side called a grandguard, to protect the face, neck and chest.

On a tilting suit, there was a mounting point for a lance rest. The lance rest helped take the weight of the lance and held it firm on impact.

The Prince Henry's armour
By the late sixteenth century, full armour was used mainly for jousts and display rather than in battle, and many suits followed the design of the fashionable clothes of the day. This flamboyant suit was made in 1608 at Greenwich near London for fourteen-year-old Prince Henry, the son of James I. Henry, who died in 1612 aged just eighteen, was very keen on military sports and may well have fought jousts in this suit.

The breastplate is pointed at the waist into a bulge known as a peascod, which was very much the fashion around 1600.

The knight's foot was protected by a series of plates called a sabaton, the lower part of his leg by a greave, the upper part by a cuisse and the knee by a series of plates called a poleyn.

The helmet was designed to fit completely over the head. The fixed back section was called the skull. The hinged plates over the face consisted of the lower bevor for the jaw, the upper bevor for the face and the visor for the eyes.

The knight's shoulder was protected by a pauldron. This was made of hinged lames (strips) of steel that allowed the shoulder to move freely.

The arm was covered by a vambrace, the elbow by a hinged plate called a cowter, and the hand by a gauntlet.

Horse armour

Horses were very expensive, but most knights had several – typically a pair of powerful destriers or warhorses for battle, a swift courser for hunting, an easygoing palfrey for travelling and a sumpter or packhorse to carry baggage. Horses were rarely fully armed, even in battle, but they often had a headpiece called a shaffron, like this one of Prince Henry's from 1610. This one was used for tilting.

From the sixteenth century on, decorations were often etched on to suits with acid. The decorations might also be gilded.

Under the armour, a knight wore a jacket of mail and leather called an arming doublet. This often had waxed thongs or points on to which the armour would be tied.

Completing the knight's armour was usually a shield (not shown here) made of wood covered in leather which was held together with metal studs which were rivet heads.

Armour pieces

All the pieces of a knight's armour were joined together in such a way that the knight could move freely and easily. Some plates are joined with a rivet that pivots, some with sliding rivets and some with leather straps. A gauntlet, for instance, might be made of a dozen or more hinged plates.

Henry VIII's armour

This huge suit of armour was made for Henry VIII in about 1539 by the armourer Erasmus Kyrkenar at the armouries Henry had set up at Greenwich, near London. This suit was not made for battle but for the joust to celebrate Henry's marriage to Anne of Cleves in 1540.

Lords and Ladies

AT FIRST, Windsor Castle was little more than a fortress. But in the 1200s, a magnificent palace was created behind the grim defences. Walls and towers were gaily painted inside, fine rooms were adorned with carpets and tapestries, and pleasant gardens were created where lords and ladies could wander.

The big event of the day in most medieval castles was the banquet in the Great Hall. Early in the morning, servants covered the long trestle tables with cloths of white linen and laid out spoons, cups and bowls. About midday, a fanfare of pipes summoned the feasters into the hall. The benches at the side table quickly filled with the lowlier courtiers. Then another fanfare heralded the entrance of the king and queen, members of the royal household and guests who were to sit at the top table. When the king sat down, he would wave his hand and the feasting could begin.

The food arrived with great ceremony. The doors opposite the king's dais swung open, trumpets blared, drums rolled, and in came a procession of servants. At their head was the marshal with his staff. Then came the cook with his wooden spoon, and finally stewards bearing food. As the food went in, a pantler tasted it to make sure it was not poisoned. It was then set on a side table where lords and knights would carve the meat and serve it to the king's table.

The great kitchen
Food was prepared in the kitchen, where cooks chopped up carcasses, and scullions, their lowly assistants, sweated over roaring fires as they turned the spits. The kitchens of most castles were just lean-tos against outside walls, because of the risk of fire. But Windsor had a large indoor kitchen as long ago as the thirteenth century.

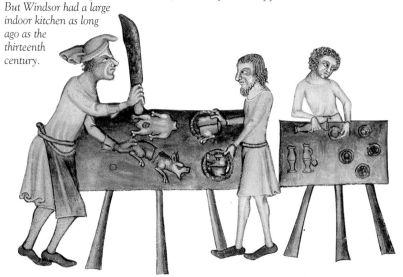

A royal feast
Medieval banquets were always noisy, with dogs barking, servants shouting and feasters making merry. The king was noisiest of all; it was his duty to be jolly. But ushers were sometimes sent round to beg the diners to hush a little.

Lesser folk sat 'below the salt' – beyond the two big salt cellars on the line of tables either side of the hall. Only a select few sat at the king's table on the dais across the top of the hall.

Diners ate meat off a trencher – a round of day-old bread like a stale pizza. After the feast, the gravy-soaked trenchers were given to the poor.

The king and queen sat on chairs, but everyone else sat on benches.

The king had his meat served on a trencher to save him fishing it out of the broth with his hands.

The king's dish was piled high with food to dole out to favoured guests.

Sometimes the king had a nef, a fully rigged ship made of silver, to hold his napkin.

Lute players wandered around gladding(entertaining) the guests, along with acrobats and jesters (comedians).

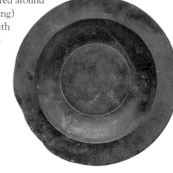

Pewter plate
Dishes, plates and cups on the top table were silver and gold, but on the lower tables they were earthenware or wood. Servants ate off pewter plates or trenchers.

Personal knives
There were no forks, and everyone had their own knife, kept in a sheath hung from the waist.

Medieval beer jug
The butler sent round young squires (would-be knights) with jugs of wine or fifteen different kinds of beer to serve the lords and ladies.

All kinds of meat were served – beef, mutton, pork, suckling pig, venison and goat as well as cranes, peacocks, swans, partridges, woodcocks and larks.

Water for diners to wash their hands was brought in bronze jugs called ewers, often elaborately shaped like a knight on horseback.

Many dishes were very elaborate, especially the subtleties – giant metre-high painted sugar, marzipan and jelly sweets made in the shape of ships, castles and hunting scenes.

People shared cups of wine and dishes of food. Younger diners served food from the dish on to trenchers for other guests and lords served ladies.

The Knight's Castle

THE REIGN OF KING EDWARD III, from 1327 to 1377, saw Windsor Castle at the height of its medieval glory. Tall, handsome and brave, Edward was a heroic figure, and his stirring victories over the French at sea at Sluys in 1340 and on land at Crécy in 1346 and Poitiers in 1356 brought English knights great fame. Edward's success also made England very rich at the expense of the French and he spent huge sums of money rebuilding Windsor Castle on a magnificent scale, making it the most fabulous castle in Europe.

Edward cherished knightly ideals – courage, skill at arms, nobility and the idea of fighting for the honour of a lady. During his reign Windsor saw many 'noble jousts and great feasts'. Knights would come from all over Europe to fight at these jousts, and enjoy the company of fair ladies, the music of minstrels, dancing, drinking and feasting.

During Edward's reign, the Inner Gatehouse was completely rebuilt with twin towers over dungeons hewn out of the chalk rock. The grooves for the heavy portcullis can still be seen.

While all the building work was going on, Edward and his queen, Philippa, stayed in the Round Tower. Wood from 170 oak trees was hauled all the way up the mound to erect a residence within the ring of stone. One remarkable feature of the Round Tower was the great clock installed in 1351. It had no face, but a huge bell chimed every hour – which must have given the King and Queen many a restless night.

By Edward's time, Windsor Castle was so rarely threatened by attack that the Round Tower moat was dry and overgrown. After 1319, five women were paid one penny a day to keep it free of nettles. Soon after it was made into a garden.

Knights had to be helped into their armour by their squire, a young nobleman training to be a knight.

Tournaments were fiercely competitive and only the bravest knights would 'enter the lists' – that is, come forward to contest. There were all kinds of contests – archery, trials of strength and fights with swords or wooden staffs. But the most spectacular were the jousts. Here two knights in full armour hurtled towards each other at full tilt on horseback and tried to knock each other down with long lances. The lances were blunted, but a fall from a horse in heavy armour could cause frightful injuries.

There were always plenty of sideshows at a tournament. You might laugh at the antics of a dancing bear or be lulled by the singing of a wandering minstrel. You might buy hot pies, beer or exotic cloths from stalls. You might even throw rotten fruit at some poor criminal in the stocks.

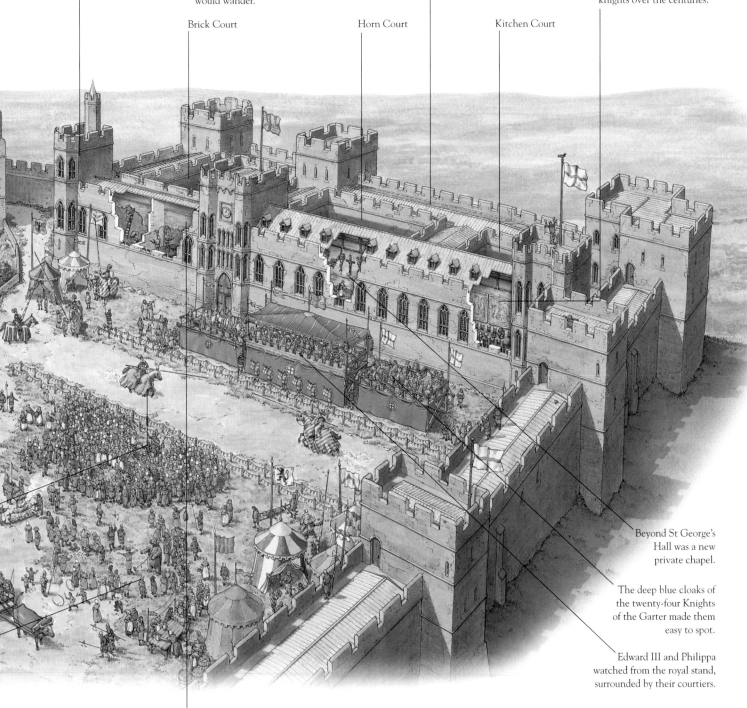

North of Brick Court were the King's five Privy rooms, where he met people in private. They were unusually sumptuous for a castle of that time. The ceilings of rooms in La Rose Tower were embossed with painted and gold-leaf roses.

New rooms were built around three quiet courtyards (later called Horn, Brick and Kitchen Courts) where neat rows of roses, gillyflowers and lavender grew. The flowers and herbs were strewn over castle floors to create a sweet smell. Around each court was a covered arcade, floored with marble, where King Edward and Queen Philippa would wander.

North of Horn Court were the King's three State rooms, where he conducted court business. These included a hall, a great chamber and a smaller hall called the painted chamber.

St George's Hall was the grandest of the new rooms. It was a lofty room with heavy oak roof beams and tall pointed windows and has remained the setting for the great banquets of the Garter knights over the centuries.

Brick Court

Horn Court

Kitchen Court

Beyond St George's Hall was a new private chapel.

The deep blue cloaks of the twenty-four Knights of the Garter made them easy to spot.

Edward III and Philippa watched from the royal stand, surrounded by their courtiers.

Building the new rooms at Windsor took thousands of tons of stone brought by horsecart and boat, 600 oak trees, over 1000 paving tiles, tons of heavy ironwork and boatloads of coloured glass.

Queen Philippa's rooms were south of Brick Court. She had a small chamber with just a bed, a hall of mirrors where she could admire herself, a chamber in which she and her maids danced, and a great chamber hung with tapestries.

EDWARD III'S CASTLE

The rebuilding of Windsor Castle began in 1359, under the supervision of Edward III's chaplain, William of Wykeham. It was a huge undertaking. 'Almost all the carpenters and masons that were of any account in the land' came to Windsor and were kept at their task for ten years. This picture shows a tournament in 1367, when the work was almost finished.

Dungeons and Damsels

THE LATE 1300S was a time when poets known as troubadours celebrated romantic love between a knight and his lady. In troubadours' tales, hearts were broken, battles fought, quests pursued, castles stormed, fair damsels (ladies) won, and songs played – all in the name of love. Such knightly tales were cherished at Windsor, home of the Knights of the Garter.

The Wife of Bath in *The Canterbury Tales*

The Physician in *The Canterbury Tales*

Of all the troubadours, the most famous was Geoffrey Chaucer (1340–1400). Chaucer was often at Windsor, and his *Knight's Tale* and *Squire's Tale* may have been written for the Garter knights' feasts at Windsor. Beautiful Criseyde in his romance *Troilus and Criseyde* is based on Joan, the Fair Maid of Kent, who married the Black Prince at Windsor. Chaucer was clerk of the King's Works as well as a poet, and in 1390 he was asked to repair the old chapel of St George at Windsor which was in a poor state. It was while carrying out these repairs that he wrote his best known collection of poems, *The Canterbury Tales*.

Captive kings

At the height of Edward III's power in the 1350s, two kings were prisoners at Windsor, David II of Scotland and John of France. They were treated well, and John often went hunting and hawking in the forest. Legend has it that while riding one day with Edward, the two captive kings urged him to rebuild the castle. After eleven years as a prisoner, David was so homesick he agreed to give up the throne of Scotland to Edward in exchange for freedom. This picture from a medieval manuscript shows David and Edward shaking hands on the deal.

PRISONERS OF LOVE

In Chaucer's *Knight's Tale*, Palamon is imprisoned in a castle tower with his cousin Arcite. One day, Palamon sees lovely Emelye in the garden below and falls in love (fifteenth-century illustration, right). As he wrote, Chaucer was probably thinking of Windsor's Devil's Tower, which overlooks the gardens of the Round Tower moat. By coincidence, the Scottish King James I was a prisoner in the Devil's Tower twenty years later. From his cell, he too saw a lovely girl walking in the gardens and fell in love. The girl later became his queen, and he wrote a poem about their love called *The King's Quair* (*quair* is scottish for book).

18

Chaucer's The Canterbury Tales

The Canterbury Tales *is the story, told in verse, of a group of pilgrims journeying from London towards Canterbury. To pass the time on the journey, which would have taken several days, each pilgrim is asked to tell a story. Chaucer completed twenty-two of the tales and a Prologue (introduction) which tells us about the pilgrims. The collection is one of the greatest series of poems ever written.*

Geoffrey Chaucer, 1340–1400

The Cook in *The Canterbury Tales*

Dangling for alms
Prisoners were obliged to pay for their own food while held captive. Poor prisoners in the Henry VIII Gate Tower (above) used to beg for donations from passers-by by dangling a bucket on a string from their cell window.

Dungeons
In the Middle Ages, noble prisoners were held in the Devil's Tower, now called the King Edward III Tower. Other prisoners were kept in the dungeon at the base of the Curfew Tower in the Lower Ward (above).

In the stocks
Some prisoners at Windsor were kept for a few days in the stocks. These held the legs and arms clamped. Passers-by pelted them with rotten vegetables.

Behind the Walls

THE HEART of a medieval castle was the great hall, the castle's main room. In the earliest castles, it was the only room, and people ate here, slept here and carried out all castle business. Later on, the lord and his lady began to cut themselves off from the other members of the court and sleep in a separate room called a bower, or a solar if it had windows to let the sun in. By the mid-thirteenth century, the great hall was just the biggest of a whole collection of rooms.

In many earlier, smaller castles all the rooms were in a single tower, called a tower-keep – the keep was the strong point defenders retreated to when the outer walls were breached. In larger castles like Windsor, the rooms were often in separate buildings within the castle walls. The great hall was the largest building, but there could be many others scattered around the castle enclosure, including the king's private chambers, stables, chapels, mews, a buttery and a kitchen. Often these were linked by covered passageways against the wall, called penthouses.

A castle wedding
With their grim stone walls and narrow window slits, castles today can look gloomy places. In fact they were often quite colourful. There were not only candles, torches and roaring fires to keep them bright and warm, but in later castles, there were also richly decorated tapestries and oriental carpets. The clothes of the richer inhabitants, too, were made of luxurious and brightly coloured fabrics, as this fifteenth-century illustration shows. It is the wedding of a French nobleman, Renaud of Montauban to his bride Clarisse.

Private stair used by the lord of the castle. Staircases were narrow and spiralled up clockwise. This meant a defender could retreat up the stairs while swinging his sword in his right hand. The attacker was hampered by the wall on his right.

Minstrels (musicians) often played soothing or cheerful music from a gallery in the main hall.

The largest room in the castle was the lord's hall on the second floor. Here people ate, slept and carried on castle business. It was sparsely furnished, with just trestle-tables and benches and candle stands. Only the lord had a chair, often made of oak and with a huge canopy.

Beneath the main hall, on the first floor, was often the garrison hall, where most of the soldiers ate and slept.

The entrance to the tower was usually on the first floor, and often across a drawbridge. This made it much harder for attackers to get in.

TOWER-KEEP
Here is a representation of a typical twelfth-century keep (although not Windsor itself), showing its main features. The keep was always the last resort in early castles, and was the heart of most smaller castles. In the Middle Ages, the keep was called a donjon, which gave us the word dungeon, since prisoners were often kept in the basement. Later on, the great hall was often a separate building.

Many rooms had running water, delivered through pipes from a rainwater cistern (tank) on the roof.

A few castles like this had extra rooms on a third floor. Here the lady had her bower, comfortably furnished with rush mats on the floor, rich wall hangings and a large bed.

Some castles had little rooms set in the thick walls, called mural chambers – one was named the garderobe: it was sometimes used as a closet for keeping clothes and valuable possessions and sometimes a toilet.

Toilets were called many things, like privy, jake, latrine and gong. But they were all just a wooden hole over a long chute dropping down into the gong-pit. People sat side by side, often three or four at a time. There was no toilet paper – handfuls of hay were used.

A water supply was vital for a castle under siege, so there was usually a well running down through the centre of the keep.

Every keep had its chapel – usually on the top floor so that there should be no structure between it and heaven.

Tower keeps were usually split in two halves by a cross-wall, which was an extra defensive barrier and a support for floor timbers.

On the first floor, there might be another chapel or the garrison's chamber, where the soldiers chatted.

Even in peacetime, the castle gates were locked at night, and visitors came in through a small door within the main doors, called a wicket gate.

Walls were very thick – two metres or more. The walls were usually a sandwich, with outer faces of neatly trimmed blocks of stone called ashlar, and a core of rubble held together with mortar.

The undercroft also held the dungeons. Sometimes these were proper strongrooms. In others they were simply the gong-pit. Worst of all was the oubliette. This was a deep, dark, dank pit into which prisoners were lowered through a trapdoor – then often forgotten (*oubliette* comes from the French for forgotten).

Surviving a siege depended on a good store of food, firewood and arms, so the store in the undercroft (basement) was kept well stocked and firmly under lock and key to prevent pilfering. Often the stores could only be entered from the lord's chamber.

Closet action

The small mural chambers of a castle provided a quiet place for the ladies of the castle to work – sewing, embroidering tapestries and sometimes painting pictures. This illustration is from the The Story of Thamyris *by the Italian writer Giovanni Boccaccio (1313–1375).*

Carpentry shop

Craftsmen of all kinds were needed in a castle, and one of the most important was the carpenter, who made everything from furniture to shields and water-butts.

In the garden

By the late fifteenth century, castles had become much more comfortable places. One popular addition was a garden where lords and ladies could wander. In this Flemish illustration, there is even a small fountain.

Who's Who

A GREAT CASTLE like Windsor was not only a fortress garrisoned by knights and soldiers, but a focus of medieval life, and it needed a lot of people to keep it running smoothly. There were not only all the king's courtiers, servants and officials – including stewards, constables, pages and ladies-in-waiting – there were also churchmen to minister for the castle's spiritual needs, jugglers, acrobats and minstrels to entertain everyone, kitchen staff to stock the castle with food and prepare the food for the table, serving men to carry food to the great hall, blacksmiths and armourers to keep the soldiers' weapons in trim, stonemasons and carpenters, laundresses, potters, physicians, clerks and many more.

Holy men
Religion played a major part in medieval life, and every castle had its own chaplains.

Menials
Every castle had its range of dirty or humble jobs such as dyer, laundress, potter and weaver. But the lowliest job of all must have been gong farmer. His job was to clean out the cesspit at the bottom of the garderobe (toilet) with a bucket and spade. Ironically, the man in charge at the top end of the garderobe, the Groom of the Stool, rose to become one of the most important figures in the royal household.

Dyer   Laundress

Windsor Castle extended over thirteen acres

Chapel

Pigsties

Dovecote

Lower Bailey

Hen-coops

Cow byres

Grooms and armourers
Keeping the soldiers equipped required a team of grooms for the horses, armourers, attiliators (crossbow makers) and blacksmiths. The blacksmith was one of the most important of all castle workers. He not only made swords and axes, but with a carpenter made all the castle's tools and carts. Tools and carts together were called deadstock – its livestock were its animals.

Groom   Armourer   Blacksmith   Attiliator
(Crossbow maker)

Carpenter   Thatcher   Master mason   Stonemason   Plumber

Builders and masons
Keeping the castle in good shape and putting up new buildings kept a small army of builders busy all the time. Thatches of straw or reeds were the cheapest roof material, so roofing outhouses called for a thatcher. The castle's many walls called for skilful stonemasons. The most important of these men was the master mason, who was basically the architect.

Tailor   Clerk   Gaoler   Gatekeeper   Physician   Ropemaker

Tailors, gaolers and others
All the castle's needs had to be catered for on the spot, so the range of skills needed was huge. Tailors made clothes. Bakers made bread. Clerks kept accounts. Physicians looked after the sick. The job of the king's own physician – or "Doctoure of Physyque" – was not only to keep him well, but to advise him on what to eat.

Spinster

Gong farmer

Page Lady-in-waiting Constable Guest Squire for the Household

Squire Knight Lord Chamberlain King Queen

The King's Chambers

The fifteenth-century Black Book of the Household shows just how many people worked at Windsor. The King's Chambers alone, for instance, were served by over 400 people, presided over by the Lord Chamberlain. Below him were the Knights for the Body, who waited on the king. Below them were the King's Knights and the Squires for the Body, who dressed the king and slept in his room.

Then came the Squires for the Household, who waited on the king's table, and Gentlemen Ushers, who made sure everyone behaved. Then there were yeomen, messengers, torch-bearers and grooms and pages (boys who took lessons in horse riding and languages, but also had to keep the floors clean). The queen, too, had her own large household, including scores of maids, and then there were all the castle's officials, presided over by the Constable.

Workshops

Court

King's Chambers

Kitchen

Upper Bailey

Stables

Farriery, where horses were shod

Blacksmith's forge

Gatehouse

Dungeon

Penthouse

Ale conner

Brewer Cook Vintner

Food and drink suppliers

Keeping the castle household supplied with food and drink was a huge task and involved hundreds of men and women. Not only were there scores of cooks and scullions in the kitchen, but also buttery men to supply butter and milk, vintners to supply wine and brewers to make beer. The ale conner made sure beer was not too sugary by sitting in a pool of it on a stool. If after an hour his leather breeches stuck to the stool, the beer was too sugary.

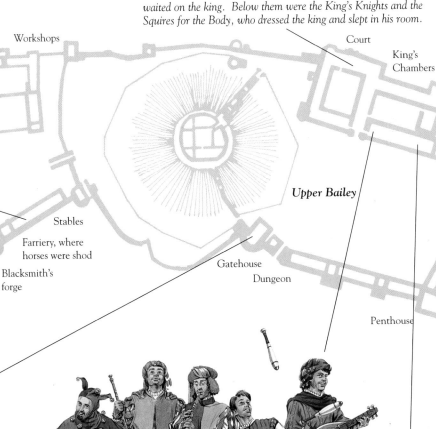

Jester

Horn player

Tabor player

Juggler

Lutanist

Entertainers

There were performers who entertained the castle guests every day – jugglers, tumblers (acrobats), knife-dancers, storytellers, minstrels and musicians. Jesters or fools held a very privileged position. They dressed in a colourful costume called motley that mocked the lords' fashionable clothes, and their job was to make fun of their masters or sing rude songs.

Table servers

Over ten thousand meals were served every day in the Great Hall, and there were scores of men to wait upon the tables. They included the butler (or bottler), who looked after the wine, the pantler, who tasted the food for poison, and trenchermen, who doled out the broth into trenchers (bread plates).

Steward

Pantler

Trencherman

Cloisters and Chapels

The Crest of the Earls of Longford

THE FIRST STONE of the great chapel of St George in Windsor Castle was laid in 1475. This was a brief time of peace in the terrible struggle for the throne of England between the warring royal families of York and Lancaster. The Yorkist king, Edward IV, had vanquished his Lancastrian rival Henry VI. Edward was anxious to show everyone that he was a god-fearing man. He sent orders to masons and carpenters of the Office of the King's Works to build him a beautiful chapel at Windsor – a burial place fit for kings and a soaring spiritual home for the Knights of the Garter. Sadly, Edward IV did not live to see his chapel completed, for he died in 1483, plunging England into war again. The chapel was finally finished in 1528, by which time Henry VIII was king.

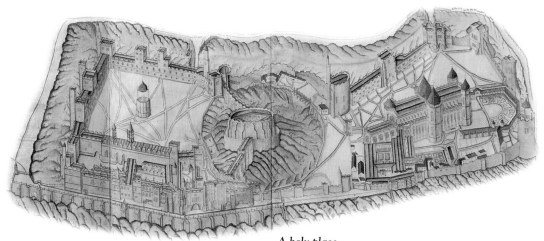

A holy place
This bird's eye view of Windsor, drawn by John Norden in 1607, shows the cluster of buildings in the Lower Ward, to the right. Ever since Edward III set up the Order of the Garter in 1348, the Lower Ward had been mainly a place of religion. Here in the Horseshoe Cloister, built for Edward III in 1351, lived twenty-six canons and minor canons and twenty-six old Poor Knights, each meant to pray for the king or one of the Garter knights.

Elizabeth and her knights
The feasts of the Garter knights are one of the great and lasting pageants of Windsor. Ironically, this elaborate picture of the 1578 celebrations with the castle in the background was commissioned by Elizabeth I – one of the few monarchs who often held Garter feasts away from Windsor.

THE GARTER KNIGHTS

Edward III founded the Order of the Garter in 1348 to set up a band of chosen knights in the spirit of King Arthur's legendary Knights of the Round Table. Originally, he planned to have 330 knights and a huge round feasting hall, but eventually decided on twenty-four special knights plus his son, the Black Prince. There have been just twenty-four Garter knights ever since, for a new knight is chosen each time one dies. Each knight has a stall in St George's Chapel.

Sir Ralph Bassett
This is the stall plate in St George's Chapel of Sir Ralph Bassett. As a young squire, Sir Ralph joined the army of the Black Prince. At the age of twenty-one, he was one of the heroes of the Battle of Poitiers in 1356. He was one of the earliest Garter knights. Edward III awarded him a knighthood in 1368.

The Nevill Family Crest
For centuries the Nevills were among the most powerful families in the country. Ten Nevills have been Knights of the Garter. They display a bull as their crest because they inherited Brancepeth Castle from a family called Bulmer.

Sir John de Mowbray
Sir John was made a Knight of the Garter by Edward IV in 1472. He was one of the leaders of Edward's disastrous invasion of France in 1475, when Edward tried to relive the glories of his namesake Edward III a hundred years earlier.

Sir Bermond Arnaud de Preissac
Sir Bermond was one of the great Gascon knights (from Gascony in France) who fought alongside the Black Prince at Poitiers. Severely wounded at the Battle of Cocherel, he recovered to become one of the heroes of English campaigns in France. He was knighted in 1379.

Sir Walter Paveley
Sir Walter Paveley was one of the original Knights of the Garter – one of the twenty-four knights who became part of the Order which Edward III founded in 1348.

ST GEORGE'S CHAPEL

In this eighteenth-century watercolour by Charles Wild, the banners of the Knights of the Garter hang above crested helmets over the canopied stalls of each Knight Companion. Beneath the floor lie the tombs of ten kings and queens of England, including those of Edward IV, his Lancastrian rival the saintly Henry VI, Henry VIII and his favourite wife Jane Seymour, Charles I, Edward VII and George VI.

Herne the Hunter

The Royal Hunt

NOTHING EXCITED the young King Henry VIII more than a day's hunting in the forest at Windsor. Fresh morning air, the first scent of the deer, the baying of the hounds, the mad gallop after their quarry, the bloody conclusion – all gave him a tremendous thrill.

Henry had boundless energy as a young man. During his time, and that of his daughter Queen Elizabeth I, Windsor became a place of enjoyment and splendour. There was hunting, shooting, hawking, riding, jousting and wrestling. There was tennis in the court built in the moat around the foot of the Round Tower. There were banquets and feasts. There was dancing and music – Henry himself played the flute and virginals and wrote songs. And there were all kinds of entertainments – plays to make the lords and ladies of the court cry and the antics of fools and jesters, of whom the most famous was Will Somers, to make them laugh.

Henry indulged in all this fun partly because he enjoyed it, but it had a serious purpose too – to impress foreign visitors with the power and luxury of the English court. Eventually, though, Henry became too fat for the more boisterous pleasures – so fat that Windsor had to be equipped with ropes and pulleys to haul him upstairs. When he died in the winter of 1547, a six-kilometre-long procession wound its way from London with the giant coffin, to bury his body in St George's Chapel at Windsor.

The young King Henry was said to throw a spear well and 'draws the bow with greater strength than any man in England'.

Lords and ladies hunted on horseback while servants ran alongside.

The stag was called the quarry, after the French *curée*. The *curée* was the ceremonial skinning of the dead animal after the hunt.

The agreeable machine
Queen Elizabeth I, who reigned from 1558 to 1603, found Windsor far too chilly in winter. She was said to complain that her dinner was always cold because it was carried all the way from the Royal Oven in the town. The Queen's maids of honour also complained because the partitions in their chamber were so low that servants could see them in bed. But Elizabeth often came down to Windsor to hunt in the summer. She slept in a giant bed nearly four metres square. She also had built a beautiful stone terrace along the north front of the castle in place of Henry's wooden wharf. At one end, she designed for herself 'an agreeable machine' – a swivelling seat with a hood that could be turned away from the wind or sun so that she might 'enjoy, even in a Storm, a perfect Calm'.

HUNTING THE HART

Ever since the days of William the Conqueror, royal forests had been set aside for the king and his companions to go hunting. Death was the penalty for anyone else caught hunting in a royal forest.

The prized target or quarry of the royal hunters was the red deer hart, a red deer stag old enough to have a magnificent crown of antlers. But they also hunted bucks (fallow deer stags) and wild boar, both of which could slit a man from knee to breast with a single stroke of their sharp tusks.

In 1533, Henry had a wooden terrace built right along the north wall, from where he could admire the lovely view, and practise shooting at a small target with his handgun.

In Tudor times, Windsor was a romantic-looking castle with tall towers, and the beauty of its setting inspired many delighted visitors.

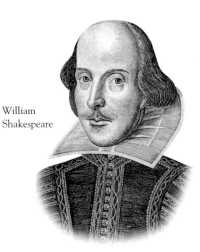

William Shakespeare

Shakespeare's Merry Wives
The great playwright William Shakespeare (1564–1616) knew Windsor well. When Queen Elizabeth I asked him to write a play for her, he set it near the castle and called it The Merry Wives of Windsor. He wrote the play in just fourteen days and it was performed in a timber-framed hall that is now the library of St George's Chapel. The Merry Wives is about a lovable rogue, Falstaff, who woos two wives, Mistress Ford and Mistress Page. The two wives get their revenge when he is beset by their neighbours disguised as fairies in Windsor Forest. For this scene, Shakespeare drew on the local legend of Herne the Hunter, a strange being who wore antlers on his head.

Mistresses Ford and Page in *The Merry Wives of Windsor*

Hounds were a vital part of the hunter's armoury. Hounds called harriers hunted by smell and were looked after on the hunt by servants called berners. Greyhounds were also used. They hunted by sight and were looked after by fewterers.

At his belt, the Master of the Hunt wore a horn that he would blow or wind (pronounced wined) to summon the hunt. During the hunt, he would blow different series of notes on the horn to signal their progress.

Henry's hunting sword
This beautiful hunting sword was made for Henry VIII in 1544 by the Spanish swordmaker Diego de Çaias. The decorations on the hilt show how the French town of Boulogne had been captured by Henry's armies earlier that year.

27

By Royal Command

Edward VI by Nicholas Hilliard

In the finished miniature portrait, Edward wears a jewel hung on a chain and decorated with the crown and feathers of the Prince of Wales. Details like this would have been added at a later stage.

IN THE MIDDLE AGES, many of the best artists painted religious scenes for churches. In 1534 King Henry VIII broke with the Church of Rome and England became Protestant. Protestants preferred their churches plain and simple, and so artists were no longer needed. Instead they began to paint portraits and landscapes for the rich and powerful – and no one was more rich and powerful than King Henry VIII himself.

From King Henry VIII's time on, the kings and queens of England began to commission the best artists to paint portraits of themselves, their family and their courtiers or to paint favourite views. The result is that royal palaces like Windsor Castle house an almost unrivalled collection of great portraits and landscapes, commissioned by the royal family through the ages.

DRAWINGS BY LEONARDO DA VINCI

Besides commanding some of the greatest painters to create pictures and paint portraits for them, the kings and queens of England began to build up a collection of paintings and drawings which is now among the world's finest – containing some of the greatest of all masterpieces. The present Royal Collection, for instance, contains a fabulous series of drawings by the Italian Renaissance artist and man of science, Leonardo da Vinci. These sketches show the Head of Leda and a cat.

Usually the final painting was finished in the artist's studio – often by his assistants – from sketches made by the artist in a brief session at the palace.

Drawings at this time were generally first made in ink or coloured chalk on paper. The final painting was painted in oil on wood panels.

THE ROYAL PORTRAIT

Prince Edward, Prince of Wales, King Henry VIII's son, was one of the first royal children to go through the ordeal of sitting still for hours to have their portrait painted. The nine-year-old Prince is shown below sitting for a portrait just before he became King Edward VI in January 1547. Experts originally thought the painter was Hans Holbein, who painted and sketched many of Henry's court. Now they believe it was a Flemish (Belgian) artist instead.

Edward VI in 1547 by an unknown artist

The drawing for the final painting would be traced on to the panel in black chalk by the artist's assistant from the artist's chalk and ink sketch.

Miniatures

In the reign of Henry VIII's daughter, Queen Elizabeth, tiny portraits called miniatures became popular. They were intended to be worn as jewellery rather than to hang on the wall as paintings. The most famous miniature painter was Nicholas Hilliard. He painted this exquisite miniature, shown here almost actual size, of Elizabeth's rival for the throne, Mary Queen of Scots.

Hans Holbein drawing

This beautiful drawing of eighteen-year-old Grace, Lady Parker, was made in black and coloured chalks by Hans Holbein in 1533. It is just one of a remarkable collection of drawings made by the German painter of King Henry VIII's courtiers after he came to live in England. For his duties as King's Painter, Holbein was paid £30 per year.

The Doomed King

THE WINTER OF 1642 saw Windsor Castle under siege for the first time in over 400 years. England was in a state of civil war. Outside the castle, bombarding it with cannon, were royalists loyal to King Charles I, sometimes called Cavaliers. Inside were those who championed Parliament against the King, sometimes known as Roundheads because of their short-cropped hair. The royalist assault on the castle failed, and as the Civil War went on, the Parliamentarians made the Round Tower at the castle their centre of operations.

By 1648, the royalist cause was lost and, three days before Christmas, King Charles I was brought to the castle under armed guard. It was a miserable Christmas, not only for Charles but for the whole of the country, since Parliament had banned all but the most sober celebrations of the festival. On 19 January 1649, Charles was taken to London for trial. Eleven days later, he was beheaded at Whitehall and his body was carried to Windsor for burial.

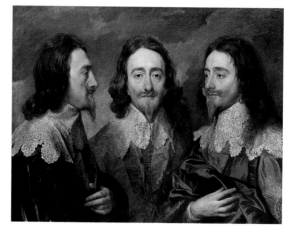

BURIAL IN THE SNOW

On 8 February 1649, Charles I's body was carried through Windsor Castle to be buried beneath St George's Chapel. It was a dismal little procession. As it moved slowly towards the chapel, snow suddenly began to fall heavily. Soon the black pall of the coffin was white with snow. It reminded people of Charles's coronation, when against all custom he wore a suit of white velvet. White was thought unlucky for a king of England, and the snowstorm was seen as an ominously fitting finale for the life of the White King.

Shirt of a doomed king?
Charles I is said to have died with great dignity. Preserved in the Royal Library at Windsor is a shirt some believe is the second shirt that Charles asked for on the morning of his execution. 'Let me have on a shirt more than usual,' the King is thought to have said, explaining that if the crowd saw him shiver in the bitter cold, they might think he was afraid. 'I fear not death,' he went on. 'Death is not terrible to me. I bless my God. I am prepared.' A boy of seventeen saw Charles's execution. Etched in the boy's memory for ever was the noise that broke from the crowd as the axe fell: 'Such a groan as I never heard before, and desire I may never hear again.'

King Charles I
Charles I, seen in this triple portrait by Vandyke, was a quiet, religious man, but he was also very obstinate. 'Men wondered that so good a man should be so bad a king', wrote the wife of one of the men who signed his death warrant. He was forever battling with his parliaments; for eleven years he ruled without one. In the end, he was tried and executed for waging war against his own kingdom and parliament.

King Charles's Shakespeare
During his final Christmas at Windsor, Charles kept up his spirits by reading sermons and the plays of Shakespeare and Jonson. This is Charles's own copy of Shakespeare's plays, with his annotations. On the flyleaf, he wrote optimistically in Latin, 'Dum spiro spero', which means 'While I breathe, I hope'.

The King's letter
Just before he went to London to be executed, Charles I signed this letter recommending his gentleman-in-waiting, Sir Thomas Herbert.

Standing in the Norman Gateway as Charles's coffin passed by was the giant porter Daniel Curtis, over two and a quarter metres tall. Daniel later became a religious maniac. Visitors to Bethlem Hospital for Lunatics often saw him dancing round with his trousers full of Bibles.

Oliver Cromwell
A man of enormous energy with a will of iron and deeply held religious views, Oliver Cromwell was the son of a squire. He came to prominence by developing the Parliamentary Army's cavalry force and leading them to victory over the royalists at Marston Moor in 1644. He was made commander of the New Model Army and led them to more victories. By the time of Charles's execution, he was the natural choice as leader of the Commonwealth which governed England instead of the king. In 1653, he made himself Lord Protector (effectively dictator) of England and remained so until his death in 1658.

The King's head
Many strange stories are attached to Charles I's relics. One of the strangest was the reopening of the vault that held his corpse on 1 April 1813. That day, people working in the vault opened the coffin and lifted out the head covered in bandages. As they unwrapped the head, they were aghast to see it intact with the left eye open and staring at them. Immediately, the eye dissolved and they were left holding the head, still wet with what appeared to be blood...

A Baroque Palace

Hugh May

IN 1660, the Commonwealth, England's brief time with no king or queen, came to an end. The country had a king again as Charles II came back from France to reclaim the throne. The people of Windsor were overjoyed, for the castle was a king's home once more after years of neglect. Charles liked coming here to play tennis, swim and fish, hunt stag, shoot birds or watch horse-races. But he found the castle old-fashioned and crude after the luxuries of French King Louis XIV's grand palace of Versailles. So he appointed the architect Hugh May to rebuild the Upper Ward of the castle as a palace in the fashionable baroque style, with high rooms, great arched windows, polished floors, and walls and ceilings covered in spectacular paintings and carvings.

The Privy Chamber was where the King held audiences with important guests, and household officers played cards.

The north front of the castle was almost completely rebuilt by Hugh May as a four-storey, flat-fronted building with high-arched windows.

The Presence Chamber was part of a series of rooms which guests had to go through before they got to the King's private chambers. Nobility and quality and their wives and daughters could watch the King sit in state in the Presence Chamber, but only a select few could progress to the next room.

Leading the string quartet was young Henry Purcell, destined to become one of England's greatest composers.

Italian music was all the rage at the time, and the King's Italian Music Consort led by Vicenzo Albrici serenaded the guests.

Nell Gwynn, the cockney actress and orange-girl who became Charles's most famous mistress

The famous diarist Samuel Pepys

The new Star Building got its name from the huge gilded
Garter Star mounted on the front. This building housed
the King's private chambers including the Withdrawing
Room, his Great Bedchamber, where he met selected
guests, and his Little Bedchamber, where he slept.

In the nest of small rooms behind the Star was
the King's lavatory, which he used before he went
to bed at night, attended by two servants – one to
hold the candle, the other to hold the paper.

The Backstairs area was where the King
relaxed in private. It was also where he met
his mistresses, brought there by his ageing
Page of the Bedchamber, Will Chiffinch.

Conveniently near at hand down the
Backstairs beneath the King's
chambers lived his favourite mistress
'Mrs Carswell', a pretty Breton girl
called Louise de Kérouaille. Charles
gave her the title Duchess of
Portsmouth.

Charles II was very interested in
science and was patron of the new
Royal Society which played a key role
in the rise of the scientific revolution
of the seventeenth century. Standing
in the background are the famous
scientists Robert Hooke and Robert
Boyle, who made important
discoveries about gases.

Also there were Hugh May and
another famous architect, Sir
Christopher Wren, a long-time
resident of Windsor, and designer of
the rebuilt St Paul's Cathedral and
many other famous buildings in
London.

WINE FOUNTAIN
This picture shows
Charles II's new palace as it
was on 30 July 1681. This
was the day that Sir Samuel
Morland demonstrated the
effectiveness of his water
engine for supplying the
palace with running water –
pumped all the way up from
the River Thames – by
shooting a fountain of red
wine mixed with water
twenty metres into the air.
The party assembled agreed
'it was the boldest and most
remarkable experiment with
water anywhere in the
world'.

Among the guests were the beautiful
Sarah Churchill and her husband the
Duke of Marlborough, who was to
become one of Britain's greatest
generals.

One of the cleaners at Windsor,
ninety-year-old Bridget Holmes, had
a special place of honour.

Sir Samuel
Morland

Charles II and his
Queen, Catherine
of Braganza

Prince Rupert, the King's cousin, was thought a wizard by the people
of Windsor. He dressed in black, went everywhere with a giant Irish
wolfhound and lived in the Round Tower, where he conducted
scientific experiments and frightened people with strange fumes.

Paintbrush and Chisel

KINGS AND QUEENS have always been able to call on the services of many of the greatest artists and craftsmen of the day – to paint pictures, to write music or stage plays, or simply to decorate their palaces. Charles II, who reigned from 1660 to 1685, was one of the great patrons of the arts. Among the artists who benefited from his interest were the composer Henry Purcell (1659–95), who became court musician, and the playwright John Dryden (1631–1700), who became Poet Laureate. During his exile in France, Charles got to know the work of many Continental artists, and in the 1670s he brought the Italian painter Antonio Verrio (1640–1707) to England to paint the ceilings and walls of the new rooms in the rebuilt Windsor. Verrio's wonderful paintings were complemented by the stunning wood carvings of Grinling Gibbons (1648–1721) and Henry Philips, and the gilding of René Cousin.

Verrio owl

Charles II by John Michael W⬛
Charles was restored to the throne ⬛ England in 1660 after more than ⬛ decade of exile in France u⬛ England was under the r⬛ Cromwell.

VERRIO'S PAINTINGS

The rich and flamboyant pictures that Verrio created at Windsor are among the masterpieces of baroque decorative art. On the ceilings, Verrio painted swirling scenes from classical myths and biblical events, but many of these fantastic figures were actually portraits of Charles, his wife Catherine of Braganza and their royal ancestors. He was also fond of including portraits of himself and his friends and enemies.

GIBBONS'S CARVINGS

Grinling Gibbons was one the greatest woodcarvers in history. He was born in Rotterdam in Holland and was a poor woodcarver in Deptford, England, until the diarist John Evelyn wandered past his tumbledown thatched cottage one day and saw him at work through the window. Evelyn took him to the King, who set him to work at once carving panels for his new palace, Windsor Castle.

The King's Dining Room

Verrio's friezes

Appropriately, Verrio painted the friezes in the King's Dining Room with a colourful array of the birds, animals and fish that might appear on the dining table. On one frieze there are ducks (above), a heron (right) and even an owl – all of which were commonly eaten at royal feasts in the seventeenth century. On another frieze (below) are a turkey, a deer for venison (already slaughtered for the table with blood dripping) and a hog's head. The frieze is given a classical look with an elaborate frame and a border of heroic figures.

The King's Dining Room

In the King's Dining Room, Verrio's paintings and Gibbons's carvings combine to magnificent effect. The doors and wall pictures – including Jacob Huysman's portrait of Catherine of Braganza – are framed by Gibbons's carvings of fruit and flowers. The ceiling and the frieze of fish and fowl are painted by Verrio.

The doorway to the King's Dining Room

A Country Park

F OR CENTURIES, kings used the Great Park at Windsor mostly for hunting. So the park keeper, called the Ranger, tried to preserve the deer and the trees that gave them shelter. But in the eighteenth century, English lords and ladies turned to quieter pleasures. Their parks became not so much something to hunt in, but something to look at, and they hired landscape gardeners to remould them into beautiful picturesque scenes. When King George III's uncle the Duke of Cumberland became Ranger in 1746, he set about turning the Great Park into a paradise of glades, woodlands and lakes dotted with romantic buildings. He created a great lake called Virginia Water and had an ornate Chinese barge made to sail on it and a little Chinese house for the boat to sail to.

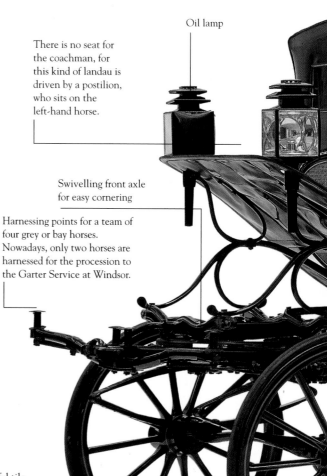

Back from hunting
After the eighteenth century, kings no longer went hunting for deer in the Great Park, but they still hunted birds, hares and rabbits. This detail from a painting by Landseer shows the young Queen Victoria greeting her husband Prince Albert after a day's shooting, with his catch laid on the stool for the house dogs and their infant daughter Vicky to play with.

Royal farmers
For George III, the Great Park was not only a place to ride, but a place to indulge one of his hobbies, farming. In 1791, he had two model farms created in the park and so earned himself the nickname Farmer George. Half a century later, Queen Victoria's husband Prince Albert did the same in the Home Park, closer to the castle. In Home Park Albert had built two handsome sets of farm buildings and an elaborate Royal Dairy. The Dairy was designed in 1858 by John Thomas and is ornamented by rows of pretty basins, painted decoration, stained glass and beautiful tilework made by the firm of Minton.

The Minton tiles in the Royal Dairy show some of the finest of all Victorian tilework.

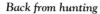
Oil lamp

There is no seat for the coachman, for this kind of landau is driven by a postilion, who sits on the left-hand horse.

Swivelling front axle for easy cornering

Harnessing points for a team of four grey or bay horses. Nowadays, only two horses are harnessed for the procession to the Garter Service at Windsor.

A beautiful tile relief showing children dressed up for country pursuits such as hunting.

Private zoo

Fat and self-indulgent, King George IV was mocked mercilessly by the press. But in the Great Park he had privacy where he could escape their taunts. He shut himself up in a giant cottage called the Royal Lodge and whiled away the time driving round the park or visiting his own private zoo. His favourite animal was a giraffe sent to him by the Pasha of Egypt. He loved his giraffe, shown here in a painting by Agasse (right). When it died, the press made fun of him for getting upset (above).

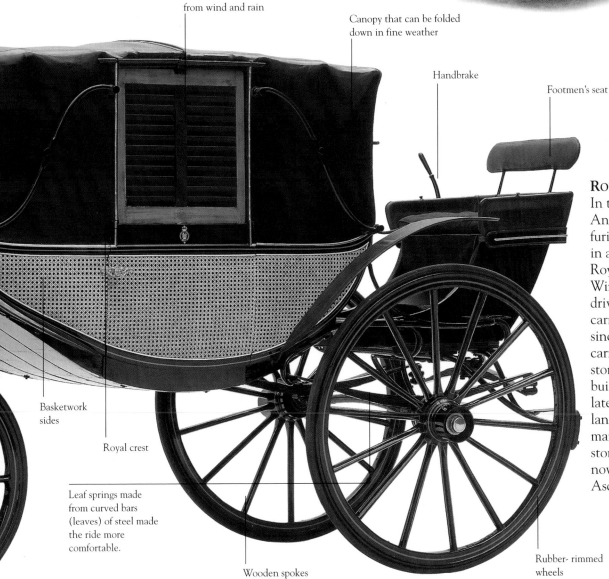

Louvred shutter for protection from wind and rain

Canopy that can be folded down in fine weather

Handbrake

Footmen's seat

Basketwork sides

Royal crest

Leaf springs made from curved bars (leaves) of steel made the ride more comfortable.

Wooden spokes

Rubber- rimmed wheels

ROYAL CARRIAGE

In the early 1700s, Queen Anne used to drive furiously around the park in a horse and chaise. Royal residents at Windsor have been driving horse-drawn carriages in the park ever since. When not in use, carriages used to be stored in the Royal Mews built by Wyatville in the late 1830s. This 1890s landau is just one of the many beautiful carriages stored there. It is used now to take the Queen to Ascot for the races.

Regal Splendour

Clock made to George III's design

Neither George I nor George II cared much for Windsor, and between 1714 and 1775 the castle fell into disrepair. But when George III took his seventeen-year-old bride Princess Charlotte there in 1761, she fell in love with it at once. Soon George and Charlotte came to live there much of the year and their friendly walks on the terrace became famous. While the castle was being renovated, they lived in a small mansion just outside the walls, called the Queen's Lodge. Sadly, before the renovations were complete George became ill with a disease called porphyria that gave him bouts of madness. But this was a time when Britain's colonies overseas were making the country very rich, and gifts began to pour into Windsor from all round the world. Treasures have continued to arrive ever since and the castle now houses a unique and priceless collection of furniture and *objets d'art*.

Queen Charlotte and her children
Like many of the women who married into the British royal family in the eighteenth century, Charlotte Sophia of Mecklenburg-Strelitz (1745–1818) was German, but she came to love England, and Windsor Castle especially. This charming picture of the Queen was painted by Gainsborough, and in Copley's picture above we see some of her fifteen children.

Inlaid cabinet
This fabulous cabinet made by the French craftsman Antoine-Louis Bellangé was bought by George IV. It is made of the dark wood ebony with gilt-bronze mounts. All over the cabinet are pictures made in pietre dure (hard stones). These are inlays of hard gemstones such as jasper and agate. The bottom two panels show almost cartoon-like pictures of two dwarfs fighting (below).

The Royal Bed

This extraordinarily ornate four-poster bed is in the King's State Bedchamber. This room was not the room the king actually slept in. In centuries gone by, the King's Bedchamber was the only place where he could conduct business in private, so the Bedchamber became a place of business. Later, kings preferred to sleep elsewhere in more privacy, but the bed remained. This bed was set here by Queen Victoria for the state visit of the French Emperor Napoleon III and his Empress Eugénie in 1855. It was probably made by the French cabinet-maker Georges Jacob.

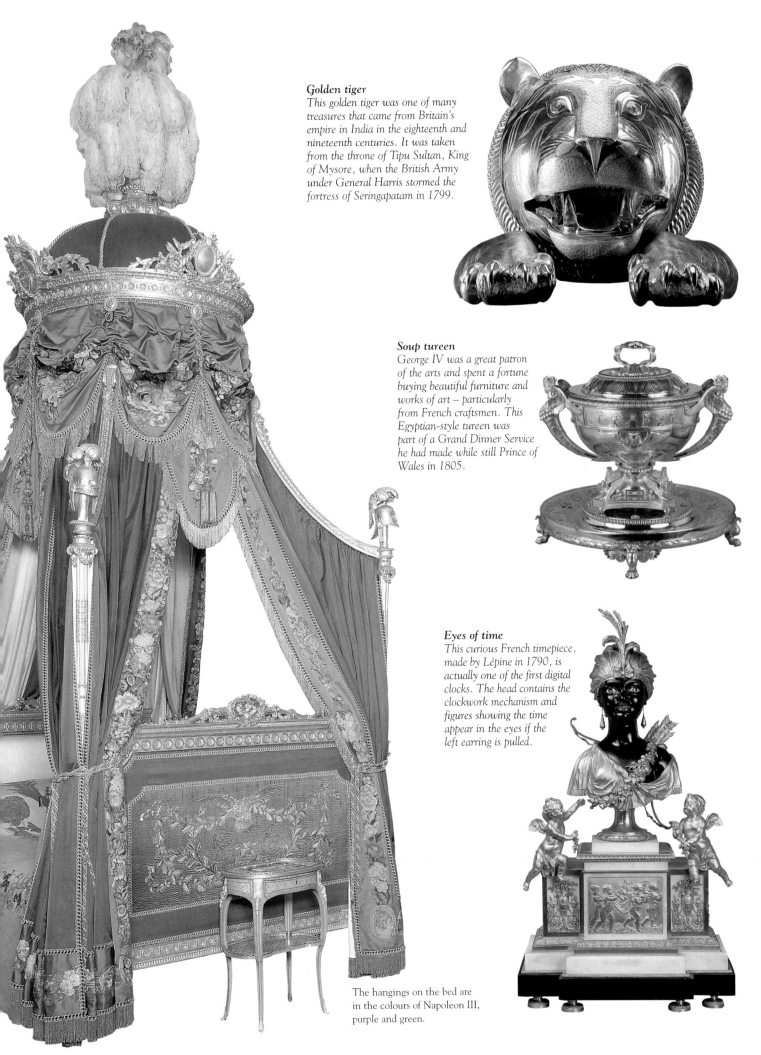

Golden tiger
This golden tiger was one of many treasures that came from Britain's empire in India in the eighteenth and nineteenth centuries. It was taken from the throne of Tipu Sultan, King of Mysore, when the British Army under General Harris stormed the fortress of Seringapatam in 1799.

Soup tureen
George IV was a great patron of the arts and spent a fortune buying beautiful furniture and works of art – particularly from French craftsmen. This Egyptian-style tureen was part of a Grand Dinner Service he had made while still Prince of Wales in 1805.

Eyes of time
This curious French timepiece, made by Lépine in 1790, is actually one of the first digital clocks. The head contains the clockwork mechanism and figures showing the time appear in the eyes if the left earring is pulled.

The hangings on the bed are in the colours of Napoleon III, purple and green.

Victorian Christmas

CHRISTMAS WAS a special time at Windsor in the 1840s. Young Queen Victoria's husband, Prince Albert, was German, and when he came to England he brought with him the German love of Christmas – and established the idea of the Christmas Tree. A picture of Victoria and Albert standing by their Christmas Tree with their two children on Christmas Eve 1841 inspired millions of English families to follow suit and bring a pine tree into their homes at Christmas.

All the rooms but the Queen's private apartments were lit by the newly installed gaslights. The Queen preferred candles.

The Christmas tree was festooned with ribbons and covered in lighted candles – so besides being beautiful it could also be a real fire hazard.

Victoria and Albert and their two children, Vicky (thirteen months) and Albert Edward (six weeks), are gathered round the tree. Prince Albert wrote to his father, 'This is the dear Christmas Eve, on which I have often listened with impatience for your step, which was to usher us into the Gift Room. Today I have two children of my own to make gifts to, who, they know not why, are full of happy wonder at the German Christmas tree and its radiant candles.'

Victoria and Albert believed in quiet family Christmases and the castle was almost empty at Christmas. The few guests are assembling in the Crimson Drawing Room for supper.

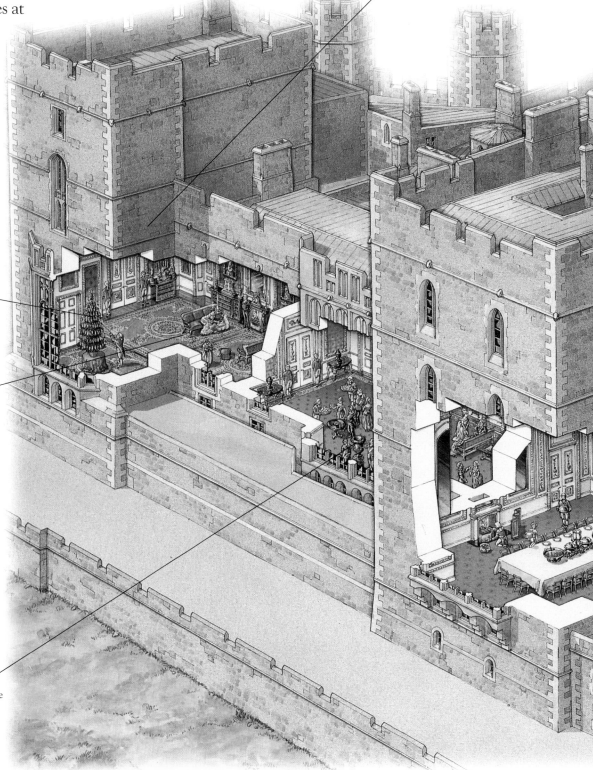

VICTORIAN WINDSOR

Just before Victoria came to the throne in 1837, the old baroque palace created in Charles II's reign had been remodelled by the architect Wyatville for King George IV. He had created a more old-fashioned gothic style, as he thought a medieval castle should look.

Wyatville's remodelling of Windsor created a number of tall medieval-style towers around the edge of the castle, each with its own narrow gothic windows.

In the scullery, scourers are hard at work, cleaning pots with sand and water.

In the green room, the vegetable cook is busy chopping up vegetables.

In the pastry room, the pastry cook is making pies and tarts.

In Victorian times four of the Great Kitchen's open fires were filled with closed ranges. But there were still giant fireplaces at either end, where a baron of beef was spit-roasted at Christmas.

The kitchen is an inferno of activity as twenty or more cooks and their assistants get to work. Spit-roasts are turned on jangling chains, dishes are scoured, plates are rushed in, pans are stirred, fires are stoked, meat is carved, oven doors are clanged …

In the centre of the kitchen was a giant shiny steel table. It was hollow and filled with steam to keep dishes piping hot.

Scottish salmon is being carefully filleted and prepared in the Fish Room.

Table-deckers prepare the table for supper, while footmen scurry to and fro bearing dishes of food from the kitchen.

In the depths of the two ancient-looking towers are the salting larder, the confectionery room, where Christmas puddings and mince pies are made, and the old plate room, where a fabulous collection of gold and silverware is kept.

Upstairs, Downstairs

William Henry Edgcumbe, Lord Chamberlain 1879–1880

LIKE EVERY WELL-TO-DO household in Britain in the nineteenth century, Windsor Castle had servants. There were over a million servants in Britain in 1851, and Windsor had at least four hundred. In some ways, Windsor was just like any other Victorian household, and the servants were divided into 'upstairs' and 'downstairs'. The finely dressed upstairs servants met guests and attended their needs; downstairs servants carried out the more manual tasks – cooking, cleaning and so on – and stayed well out of sight. But Windsor was a royal palace and the upstairs staff were not just hired servants: they were members of the Queen's Household, noblemen and women seen fit to attend the Queen.

When Queen Victoria's husband, Prince Albert, came to Windsor, he found the household very badly organized and in his typical fashion set about making it more efficient. But he made himself quite unpopular by clamping down on the perks of the job, such as free candles, and there are many caricatures of him ferreting out candle-ends.

DOWNSTAIRS

The downstairs staff were controlled by the Lord Steward. These were the servants who worked in the warren of rooms on the ground floor, below the State Apartments, and they all ate together in the Servants' Hall. Everything was strictly regulated, and there were lists of strict rules pinned up in each room instructing servants how to carry out their duties and warning them against using the wrong materials or tools for the job.

UPSTAIRS

The upstairs staff were presided over by the Lord Chamberlain. They were usually lords and ladies and could therefore mingle with the royal family, often taking part in theatricals with the children – something the downstairs staff could never do.

The elite of the Queen's household were her private staff – the Keeper of the Privy Purse, her Private Secretary and her physician.

The Ladies of the Bedchamber and Maids of Honour were young women of noble birth personally invited to be the Queen's companions. It was the Queen's dressers and lady's maids who looked after her clothes and dressed her.

There were thirty-five or more kitchen staff, and they had their own strict hierarchy. At the top of the tree was the Chief Cook with his four cooks beneath him. Then came six apprentice cooks and pastry cooks. Then finally came the kitchen maids and scourers, responsible for keeping everything clean.

The servants of the steward's room were the aristocrats of the downstairs servants. They ate in their own hall and were as finely dressed as many of the upstairs servants.

The jobs of the Gentlemen of the Wine Cellar and the Yeomen of the Pantry were to look after the wine cellar and the silverware respectively. The Yeomen of the Pantry and their seven burly helpers were responsible for gold and silver plate worth over £3m even in the 1890s. It was kept in two plate pantries which had iron doors. Five table-deckers laid and arranged the tables.

Looking after all the State Apartments, keeping them clean and providing guests with clean linen, laundry and so on, was a small army of maids – thirty-four housemaids, two linen-room maids, three coffee-room maids, numerous cleaners and four state-room attendants.

Looking after the valuable furnishings and fittings at Windsor and keeping them in perfect condition required a large staff of skilled craftsmen – upholsterers, cabinet makers, joiners, French polishers, japanners, gilders, needlewomen and so on.

Besides a variety of pages, Queen Victoria had various Highland servants – brought from her Scottish home in Balmoral – and Indian servants, including her Indian secretary, Munshi, reflecting the fact that she was not only Queen of Britain, but also Empress of India.

Over a hundred horses were kept in the Royal Mews, Windsor's stables, along with dozens of coaches. Looking after all these were twenty-five grooms, eight stablemen, four coachmen, four postilions and an outrider – not to mention the sergeant farrier and the mews keeper.

OUTSIDE STAFF

Besides the household servants, Windsor Castle employed a huge number of staff to look after the horses, maintain the coaches and drive the Queen and her guests around the park and out on state occasions. These people who worked in the Royal Mews were all presided over by the Master of the Horse.

Looking after the castle building and its grounds were scores of employees such as carpenters, plumbers, builders, gardeners, dairymaids and so on.

The Wonderful Gift

IN 1925 Queen Mary, wife of King George V, was given 'the most perfect present anyone could receive' – the most wonderful doll's house in the world, designed by Sir Edwin Lutyens, the greatest architect of the time, and fitted out in amazing miniature detail by 1500 tradesmen, artists and authors. It was shown briefly at the Wembley Exhibition of 1924, then moved to a specially converted room in Windsor Castle, where it has stayed ever since.

The beautiful classical exterior of the house is one of Lutyens's masterpieces. Made of wood, carved and painted to look like Portland stone, it can be raised to reveal the exquisitely detailed interior. Every item inside the house is a miniature marvel – exact replicas of the real thing, one-twelfth as big. Each room is fitted out just like a real room, with details down to tiny working matches or bottles filled with vintage wine. Working lifts stop at each floor, there is running water in all five bathrooms and electric lighting everywhere.

Little smoke
Pipes, tobacco and matches that lit were all made to scale. The mini matchbox was the size of a full-size match head (shown below left).

Pottery model
One of the aims of building the doll's house was to raise money for Queen Mary's favourite charities. At the Wembley Exhibition, thousands of these pottery replicas of the doll's house were sold and the proceeds donated to charity. To this day proceeds from the visitors to The Doll's House are still given to charity.

THE DAY NURSERY

This room is a perfect replica of the kind of room where the privileged children of the day spent their lives, ruled over by a nanny and out of sight of the rest of the house. It is full of amazing miniature toys – a working toy theatre, tiny soft animals, books, a train set and much more.

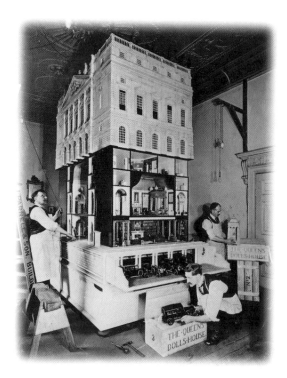

Moving house
The house was put together in the drawing room of Lutyens's house in Mansfield Street, London, supervised by Lutyens and his thirteen-year-old daughter Mary. When it was complete, it was packed up in cases labelled 'The Queen's Doll's House' and carted off to Wembley.

Tiny sounds
The tiny gramophone player actually works. It can be wound up to play little records just two and a half centimetres across. Tunes include the British national anthem, 'Rule, Britannia!' and 'Home Sweet Home'.

THE LIBRARY

The library is home to some of the house's greatest treasures, including beautiful miniature paintings, sketches and watercolours.

Mini books

The library's collection of books includes not only minute printed versions of all of Shakespeare's works, but books especially written for the miniature library by famous authors of the day, such as Arthur Conan Doyle, Rudyard Kipling and A.A. Milne. Many of these books are in their author's own handwriting and are illustrated with specially drawn pictures.

Small world

Like a full-size library, the doll's house has a globe, along with atlases, newspapers, magazines and many other reference works.

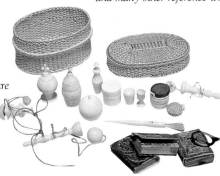

Rocking dolls

These little dolls, in their minute wicker cradle, typical of the time, are little bigger than a thumbnail – just one centimetre long.

Tiny tops

This collection of tops and skipping ropes looks just like the real thing – but the tops are smaller than a match head and the skipping 'rope' is thinner than cotton.

St George's Hall before the fire

The Fire

AT 11.30 on the morning of 20 November 1992 Windsor Castle caught fire. The blaze started in the castle's small private chapel – probably caused by curtains being too close to an electric light. Before anyone could see, the flames spread into the ceiling and began to race through the timber-framed roof. By the time the fire engines arrived, parts of the north-east corner of the castle were in the fire's grip, and all the fire brigade could do was stop it spreading much further. The fire burned all through the night, with roaring flames lighting up the sky like a medieval beacon. Volunteers and castle staff worked furiously to clear the endangered rooms of their priceless contents – and everything from Agra carpets to antique chairs piled up in the Upper Ward. By a stroke of luck, many of the most valuable items had already been removed while the rooms were rewired, and remarkably few were destroyed. The damage to the building's ancient fabric, though, was severe. By the time the fire finally burned itself out, many wonderful rooms had been devastated – the private chapel, St George's Hall, the Grand Reception Room, the Crimson Drawing Room, the State Dining Room, the Great Kitchen, and many others. Within days, however, restoration work was under way.

St George's Hall
One of the worst damaged rooms was St George's Hall, the feasting-place of the Garter Knights since the fourteenth century. Restorers decided to take the opportunity to make improvements. The ceiling destroyed during the fire had been rather low, so restorers have replaced it with a loftier one with wonderful new carved oak timbers. Above this is a new roof supported by steel girders.

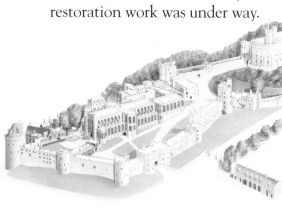

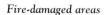

Fire-damaged areas
The fire started in the private chapel in the north-east corner of the castle, just beyond the east end of St George's Hall. Flames engulfed all the rooms in that part of the castle, including all the great reception rooms, and roared up through the Brunswick and Prince of Wales Towers as if they were chimneys. St George's Hall and the Great Kitchen were also completely gutted.

Archaeological revelations
By burning away some of the fabric, the fire revealed parts of the castle that had stayed hidden for centuries and led to a number of remarkable archaeological finds. The Great Kitchen roof, for example, was much older than previously thought. Medieval masonry was found in the Kitchen Court and fifteenth-century timbers in the roof, while a fifteenth-century rubbish pit was found to contain the remains of fifteen types of fish and meat and over thirty types of fruit and vegetable. Even more exciting was the discovery of a forty-metre-deep well near the Kitchen, dating back to the very earliest days of the castle in the thirteenth century, and traces of a portcullis groove, revealing the castle's medieval service entrance.

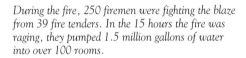

St George's Hall after the fire, above left, and above as it will appear after restoration

The Crimson Drawing Room
One of the most difficult tasks facing the restorers in the Crimson Drawing Room and the Grand Reception Room was repairing the elaborate moulded plaster ceilings. These ceilings had collapsed and smashed to the floor in thousands of pieces, so plasterers had to sift through all these fragments to find any pieces that could be recovered. Where pieces were damaged beyond repair, new pieces were made from moulds taken from pieces remaining intact. Then all these pieces, both old and new, had to be replaced with infinite care on to the ceiling, like an incredibly complex jigsaw.

During the fire, 250 firemen were fighting the blaze from 39 fire tenders. In the 15 hours the fire was raging, they pumped 1.5 million gallons of water into over 100 rooms.

Recovered plaster fragments

Restoring the plasterwork

RESTORATION WORK
Repairing the damage is a massive task but the repairs are very well advanced. With such a unique historical building, restorers had to take immense care not to lose anything which could viably be restored. So restoration work began with the painstaking removal of over 200 tons of debris. Over 7000 dustbins and 2000 breadbaskets were methodically filled with over 15,000 carefully retrieved fragments from small pieces of plasterwork to charred slivers of medieval timber – each carefully labelled so that restorers knew where they had come from. Then scaffolders erected over 130km of scaffolding. Pumps and driers were brought in to dry out fabric sodden by the fire hoses, and restoration work began in earnest.

Index

Geometricall Paſes, of 5 Feet.